That's My DJ

That's My DJ

A FAMILY'S JOURNEY WITH
AN AUTISTIC CHILD

Cindy and Michael Mayhew

ISBN: 1516870964
ISBN 13: 9781516870967

PROLOGUE

by Michael

PRANCING AROUND THE HOUSE IN a pair of comfortable plaid boxer shorts and a light blue polo shirt that's two sizes too big for his thin, Nestle-Crunch frame, twelve-year-old DJ is on another sweet-tooth mission. For the third—maybe eighth—time this week, Cindy has hid the bag of Chips Ahoy cookies, and DJ's determined to sneak around and find them.

He thinks nobody is watching, but I can see him.

But to be honest, sometimes I don't.

This kid has a way of now you see me…now you don't. On this particular day, I can see DJ checking all the closets and nonchalantly looking around for that blue bag of deliciousness he's been craving. Fortunately, DJ doesn't know his favorite Reese's Peanut Butter Cups are hidden in the trunk of my car, or he would have been kidnapped those and held them in his stomach for ransom.

DJ's allowed to eat sweets, but he still has to learn not to overindulge. Most kids will learn this the hard way by ending up with a severe tummy ache. Unfortunately, DJ has had his share of tummy aches. And the kid still thinks it's cool to eat twenty-four Reese's Cups in ten minutes or less.

So we have to save him from himself.

As DJ rabidly searches each cabinet and then quietly opens the refrigerator door, I yell, "DJ, sit down". That's when Mr. I'm-Not-Doing-Anything casually strolls back into the living room like it was all in *my* imagination.

I've finally noticed that DJ never leaves the room during the boring commercial breaks. He methodically calculates his moves during the good movie scenes when my mouth is wide open and my eyes are glued to the boob tube. If I was as smart when I was twelve years old as DJ is now, I would have skipped grade school and joined the CIA.

Since I know DJ's not going to relax until he gets his fair dose of artificial flavors and sugar, I kindly ask him to have a seat in the living room while I go and fetch a few cookies. When I return with the goods, DJ just laughs like he broke me down, grabs the cookies, and nibbles on them like he's been waiting for this moment all his life. I always get a kick out of the way DJ closes his eyes when he eats something delicious.

I envy him. I wish chocolate-chip cookies could bring me that type of joy. This is usually the time I play DJ's favorite song, "Go DJ," by Lil Wayne. Well, who am I kidding? It's actually my favorite song for DJ.

Anytime I see DJ on the prowl, I hear that song in my head:

"Cuz that's my DJ."

To be a good father and mother requires that the parents defer many of their own needs and desires in favor of the needs of their children. As a consequence of this sacrifice, conscientious parents develop a nobility of character and learn to put into practice the selfless truths taught by the Savior Himself.

James E. Faust

CHAPTER 1

Cindy—DJ's Eyes

$\mathscr{A}$fter several months of soothing heartburn
with milk and three hours of intense la-
bor, I gave birth to Desmond Winston Joseph
at Portsmouth Naval Hospital in Portsmouth,
Virginia, on December 29, 2002.

Seven lucky days after my birthday...

All my children had bushy hair when they were
born, so it didn't surprise me when DJ was deliv-
ered with a head full of brown, curly locks. I still
remember looking at my first son's big, mahogany
eyes. DJ has the kind of eyes that make you want to
smile at the world. I almost didn't want to let the
little boy go, but the nurses needed to clean him
up and do all the routine things that the hospital
required.

I don't remember hearing DJ cry.

I know my daughters, Imani and Nia, cried when
they were born.

DJ was much quieter.

At the time, I figured boys made less noise at birth. At least that's what I thought.

By the time I brought DJ home, I was already the true definition of a single mother. DJ's father (my ex-husband) and I were recently separated, and I was pretty much raising my children on my own. It's not like DJ wasn't carefully planned—I was happily married when I conceived him. I guess my marriage wasn't written in stone, and DJ's future was now solely in my hands.

My oldest daughter, Imani, was my rock at the time. At seven years old, she was Mommy's favorite helper. Imani made sure DJ always had a fresh diaper—that was her main concern. She also helped with other things, like bathing, getting bottles, and holding him while I cleaned the house. But if that diaper wasn't changed, then Imani would bring it to my attention immediately. My youngest daughter, Nia, was only four at the time. She was also a helpful child; I just had to make sure Ms. Busybody wasn't making her own mess. If ever a single parent had the perfect family, I did. I had a wonderful older daughter, a vibrant younger daughter, and my beautiful son, DJ. We became a team that was headed for the proudest family playoffs.

CHAPTER 2

Cindy — Bills

THEY DON'T CALL THEM BILLS for nothing. When bills start to build up, they become this granite wall that can't be climbed over. Here I am busting my butt trying to feed and clothe my three children, and I can barely keep the lights on thanks to my backstabbing car note. I was seriously making car payments for a hooptie that spent more time in the shop than on the road. This is America, so of course we all have bills and responsibilities. By the same token, I didn't make these kids alone, and I needed some assistance. Imani's so-called father was nowhere to be found, and getting him to support his daughter seemed *unicornish* and beyond belief. However, my ex-husband wasn't getting off the hook that easy. I had two children for him, and it wasn't fair that I wasn't receiving anything—not even a phone call. I eventually went to court and filed those child-support papers. I'm not one of those women that like to use the court system to my advantage, but I'm definitely not the type of person that likes to be taken advantage of. Papers served...

Besides, I had a beautiful son that wasn't being acknowledged by his father. All my kids deserved their rightful attention. And silly me, I figured any real man would want to be there for his only son. I guess I was wrong. I also refused to be wrong and struggling. Papers served…

After my marriage went to hell, I was determined to solely focus on my kids and find a job, career, or something to at least survive on. Most of the places that were hiring were only part-time, and I didn't have part-time bills. I needed full-time money. I eventually started working two temporary telemarketing jobs I found online. Now I was working more than spending time with my family. And this is when my family needed me the most.

It was 2004 and DJ was two years old. Up until now he was behaving like a regular child. He wasn't really talking much, but he would at least utter words like "ma-ma," "da-da," "cookie," or even say the word "no."

Suddenly he stopped talking all together.

One day, DJ's day-care teacher advised me to have DJ checked out for autism. I swear I didn't know what the hell this lady was yapping about.

When she tried to explain DJ's symptoms I nearly cussed the poor woman out.

Nothing was wrong with my child; she was probably the one that needed some damn help. Just out of curiosity and concern, I had DJ seen by a specialist for a neurological evaluation.

CHAPTER 3

Cindy—Reality

THE WORST THING ABOUT REALITY is that sometimes it's so bad that it doesn't feel real. When the doctors at the Norfolk Children's Hospital told me DJ had a neurodevelopmental disorder, I almost went into shock. I couldn't hear all the details because my heart was breaking so loudly, I thought my chest was going to collapse. These people were seriously trying to tell me that my baby wasn't normal. At least that's what I thought they were trying to tell me. I just wanted my son to have a regular chance at life like I was blessed enough to have—like other folks were blessed to have. Now these doctors were telling me that my child might never speak or interact with other people in a normal fashion for the rest of his life. I literally wanted to scream!

Thank God for the Internet. It took a lot of time consuming research to grasp everything that was happening to DJ. I had to study everything that I could about autism. I guess deep down inside I was also looking for a cure. I was praying that there was some form of medication that would eventually get DJ on the right path. Of course there wasn't any cure, just vague information on how to deal with the situation.

I wanted CT scans, MRIs or something to explain why my baby wouldn't look me in my eyes. I began to wonder if vaccines or questionable needles had something to do with DJ's condition. Someone online mentioned that a mutation of the methylenetetrahydrofolate reductase (MTHFR) gene might cause autism.

…maybe.

None of DJ's doctors mentioned MTHFR, so I was at a loss.

Autism has such a wide spectrum that I wasn't sure if that's what caused DJ's particular disorder. I didn't want to make matters worse by *chemically detoxing* him.

Even with America's most advanced medical technology, no one could explain or guarantee a damn thing.

Wow.

Then one day I woke up and realized that I had spent almost a year worrying about DJ's autism instead of simply enjoying his presence.

On DJ's third birthday I ordered a custom-made buttercream Spiderman cake and brought it to his school. At the time, DJ was still going to the same day care that he attended before he was diagnosed with autism. One of his doctors suggested that I put DJ in a program for special needs children. To hell with that! I didn't want DJ in any special programs. Besides, watching DJ interact with his classmates gave me faith that he would grow up just as normal as they were. I watched my son playfully put his little hand in his birthday cake, and all his classmates laughed as they did the same thing. See, DJ was just like all the other kids. A part of me was still in denial, and I cried every time I thought about the worst case scenario.

My eyelashes were raining black tears of sorrow as I snapped each photo. I eventually asked DJ's teacher to take the rest of the pictures. I was crying way too much.

Between hurt, confusion, and vulnerability, I didn't see the next obstacle in my life. I hadn't dated another man since my ex-husband, and to be honest, I wasn't looking for any male companionship. When Calvin introduced himself, I really wasn't interested…at all.

After all, was Calvin going to make my life better or help me cope with my autistic son? Or was he just trying to have his share of fun?

I didn't know; I didn't care.

I just needed my space.

But let's be real, it's obvious that I ended up dating him or he wouldn't be worth mentioning. Calvin was all right, even though; he wasn't exactly my ideal boyfriend.

Nevertheless, he was thoughtful and caring. Well, at least at the time. My main concern was that he understood my son's condition and he seemed eager to help make our situation better. Whatever that meant.

I must say, Calvin wasn't leading me on. He turned out to be a nice guy and we had some interesting times together. Looking back, I think Calvin wanted to be a permanent part of my family.

I was the more reluctant one.

Despite the fact that Calvin was thoughtful with my kids, especially DJ, I just wasn't in love with Calvin. I admired what he stood for. At this stage of my life I wasn't trying to marry a man that didn't captivate my heart. I had already been down that road, and it was a little too bumpy for comfort.

Calvin must have sensed that our relationship wasn't progressing. He didn't mind helping out with the kids as long as he was getting his fair share of my affection. Once he realized that I was almost at my peak, he started trying to see other females behind my back.

Of course I went the hell off!

I mean, really?

Even though I was a little reluctant to take our relationship to the next level, I was still committed and faithful to the relationship that we did have. I wasn't even the one that asked this messy dude to be in my life. Cindy was doing just fine by herself. That was pretty much the last straw. I let Calvin go do his thing and I put my own plan in motion.

I had finally convinced my ex-husband to take more responsibility for his kids. Sadly enough, he wasn't as eager as I felt he should have been. After some stern reasoning, he ultimately stepped up to the plate and allowed Imani, Nia, and DJ to stay with him and his new girlfriend. And I really needed that at the time. My sister had informed me about an exciting job opportunity working on cruise ships and making a reasonable income. Only one thing: It required me to go to Piney Point, Maryland, for a couple of months. I honestly didn't want to take a job that would literally take me away from my kids. After some deep meditation and hopeless pondering I decided this was in our family's best interest. It was just becoming too impossible to pay my bills, even with two jobs. At this rate, I was going to lose one way or the other.

The day before I left for Maryland, I locked myself in the bedroom, pushed my packed suitcases off the bed and held DJ in my arms like there was no tomorrow. I mean I really felt like there was no tomorrow. Leaving DJ behind was almost as heartbreaking as finding out that he was unable to talk. The guilt that consumed me was unbearable. I wished to God that I could find a job locally that was at least paying more than minimum wage. When I woke up the next morning, my prayers had gone unanswered and it was officially time for me to go.

I dropped off the kids at their father's house, kissed DJ good-bye, and turned him over to Imani. Even though all the kids were staying with my ex-husband, I was really depending on Imani to watch over DJ. Imani's basically the only person in the world that I trust with my son. One more final kiss. *tears*

CHAPTER 4

Imani—Deep water

⚭

THE SUMMER WAS HERE, MOMMY was gone, and I was technically in charge of DJ. And, I guess to some degree, Nia. We were staying with Nia's father, but somehow I knew DJ would be my responsibility.

It was cool...I love DJ.

DJ's like my kindred spirit. We've practically shared the same bed since he was a year old. The way DJ follows me around, I'm not sure if he's scared to be alone or if he just wants to protect his big sister. In any case, that's my DJ.

So where was I? Oh yeah...the summer had just started, and it was sizzling hot outside. I had a feeling it would be a long, crucial heat wave without Mommy around. Oh well, no sense in worrying about it, I thought. I figured we'd just make the best of things. The pool had finally opened, so I decided to take Nia and DJ swimming.

Since I can't swim, I normally keep my butt at the shallow end of the pool where it's safe. Before I could get one toe in the water, I hear this ridiculous splash and realized Daredevil DJ had jumped in the deep end of the pool.

Naturally, I panicked and ran over to the deep end!

I don't think I gave it much thought. I closed my eyes, quickly dove in the water, and went to rescue my little brother. At this time, DJ was still laughing as he managed to stay afloat of the sky-blue water. He didn't seem to realize that he was just splashing around and not going anywhere. To my surprise, I actually *was* swimming—chlorine had my eyes burning all the way back to safety. By the time we reached the 3ft end of the pool, I was a bona fide lifeguard.

It's amazing what the human body can do when there's an emergency. I was able to swim and get my brother; however, when I tried to swim on my own accord I couldn't do it. I didn't officially learn how to swim until I was fifteen. DJ was my first lesson on how to deal with a real crisis.

CHAPTER 5

Cindy—NCL

(Norwegian Cruise Line)

WHEN I ARRIVED IN MARYLAND I was a total freaking mess. I think I cried the entire flight. I felt like I hadn't seen my kids in days, and I had just left them one hundred and sixteen minutes ago.

You can do this Cindy, I kept reminding myself.

All along this paranoid feeling was swan-dancing in the back of my mind. What if this NCL gig didn't work out? Then what?

There were about five or six other recruits that were heading to the NCL (Norwegian Cruise Line) base in Piney Point. The bright-white NCL bus came and picked us all up at the airport, and it was time to let the games begin. Most of us were females; maybe two guys were in our bus group. My sister already told me that the NCL base mainly consisted of white females, a few black females, and a handful of guys.

Overall, they had a great party atmosphere. After all, we were training to serve on a cruise ship, so it would be our job to be upbeat and happy. I wasn't exactly in the party mood, but I planned to make the best of this crappy situation.

We arrived at the base later that evening and I was *so* happy to see my younger sister Tonya! She had already been at the base for two weeks and I hadn't seen her since she left Virginia. Tonya gave me the biggest hug ever and finally let me go long enough so she could introduce me to everybody she knew. Afterward, I got settled into my room, put on my gaudy Hawaiian cruise shirt, and the managers of the base took us on a quick tour.

Basically, the NCL base was set up like a hotel. We would be training for different positions on a cruise ship. I was assigned to the housekeeping department, so I would be in charge of cleaning the rooms. Now, on the other side of the base was the SIU (Seafarers International Union). That's where the *blue boys* were...*lol.* The SIU were the guys that trained to become Merchant Marines...a whole other field than NCL. The two organizations shared a base for whatever reason, and they coexisted without bothering one another. Anyway, as I was going on my tour I noticed a lot of the Merchant Marine guys were staring at us. I guess the NCL and SIU weren't allowed to fraternize. Of course, that only made them fraternize even harder. The last thing on my mind was meeting any guys, so I spent most of my time avoiding eye contact with the Merchant Marine dudes...then I noticed one guy that sorta' caught my attention.

CHAPTER 6

Cindy — Who's he?

WHEN I FIRST SAW MICHAEL I thought he was cute, but if you let *him* tell the story, I fell in love with him at first sight…*ha ha, in your dreams, buddy.* I will admit that I wanted to get to know him better. So when he actually approached me I was very interested in hearing what he had to say. To make a long story short, we had a lot in common. We were both from up north: I once lived in Brooklyn, NY, and Michael was from East Orange, New Jersey. I was actually born in Barbados and, strangely enough, his family was from Barbados. After that, we just kept getting more familiar with each other.

Before anything became serious, I basically told Michael my whole life story. I let him know that I was once married and that I currently had three children. He didn't seem too fazed or surprised by it.

So I continued…

I also let Michael know that I was recently in a bad relationship and that's why I wasn't really looking for anybody to get serious with. Maybe he understood or was just going through the motions of getting to know me.

He took everything I said with a grain of salt and we became pretty close friends.

CHAPTER 7

Michael—Who's she?

—ᜃᜃ—

WHEN I FIRST MET CINDY, she was staring at me like I was a futuristic candy bar. I mean, Shorty could barely say hello when I approached her. It was the summer of 2006; I was thirty-two years old and in the best shape of my life. Not to mention, I had a promising career as a Merchant Marine. Once I finished training I'd be making plenty of money and traveling the world. Yeah, my future was brighter than a yellow dwarf that orbits the earth.

But seriously, I noticed Cindy first, and I just felt the need to approach her. She had this carefree spirit about her that made me feel carefree.

I was actually shocked when she told me she had three kids ages eleven, nine, and four. Her body looked like a twenty-year-old centerfold model's…

…if you're into that sorta' thing.

No lie: Cindy spent at least four hours telling me about her life, and all I could think about was how *hot* she was. When we finally had our moment together, I thought it was dope. However, I didn't plan on being in a relationship with her. Truthfully, I didn't think I'd ever see her pretty face again after I left SIU training. I departed Piney Point July 15, 2006, and was headed for Hawaii to get my necessary sea time on the NCL ship Pride of America.

CHAPTER 8

Michael/Cindy —

Who are we?

‑⊰⊱‑

M: LMAO. So, please tell me why Cindy followed me on the Pride of America ship.

C: First of all, I didn't follow you. I was assigned to the Pride of America. Get it right! Ha ha...

M: No, you weren't; you were assigned to the Pride of Hawaii ship, and you had your orders changed to my ship.

C: How you gonna' tell me what I had changed? Were you my assignment leader?

M: Anyway, somehow Cindy was able to get her orders changed to the same ship that I was working on. Therefore, we not only became boyfriend and girlfriend, she somehow managed to get pregnant.

C: Really, Michael? Managed?

M: You know what I mean: Cindy became pregnant, and after two months of trying to hang in there she eventually had to leave the ship on maternity leave. So I basically went from a bachelor with no kids to a future baby daddy overnight. I was still focused on becoming a Merchant Marine, but my life was now changed forever.

CHAPTER 9

Cindy — Back in Virginia

I DIDN'T MEAN TO RUSH past Imani and Nia...

...it's just that DJ had gotten so big!

An inch may not be considered much of a growth spurt—*or at least I don't think it is.* Somehow my little peanut butter cup looked so much bigger than the last time I saw him.

I took a brief moment to look in DJ's eyes for something different—maybe a deliberate glance or a sign of affection to say that he missed his mommy. Even though DJ didn't express his emotions, I still felt he had to miss me. I sure missed the hell out of him.

I finally gave my other two boogers a hug and made my way inside the house. They were both filling me in about their summer festivies, and all the moments I regrettably missed out on.

So, apparently Imani had sunburn, Nia claimed she had died of boredom, and DJ had jumped in the deep end of the pool...

...*What!?*

Nobody mentioned DJ jumping in the pool when I was calling home every night, so I didn't understand why I was just hearing about this now.

Before I could *go off* about DJ, my ex-husband slithered inside the living room and assured me that everything was fine—*let him tell it.*

DJ looked awesome and that's all that mattered. I rolled my eyes, brushed it off, and told the kids to get their clothes together. And to make sure they had everything…

…we were going home.

I breathed a sigh of relief once we left that other house. The kids and I hopped in my old hooptie truck, turned on the radio, and rocked out to some classic Caribbean music. This became the right time to tell my daughters I was pregnant.

Imani didn't seem surprised…and Nia claimed she was moving in with her grandmother.

Lol…whatever.

DJ took the news pretty well, and that's all that mattered.

I also had another surprise. In two weeks I was going to pick up my new boyfriend from the airport.

"Boyfriend," Imani smiled at me, puzzled, as if I wasn't supposed to use *boy* and *friend* in the same context.

I simply smiled. "His name's Michael."

And little did Michael know that I had already rented a car and made plans to pick him up from New Jersey when he left the Pride of America.

We were about to be a real family, not some distant relation-ship passing each other in the middle of the night. No, sweetie, a real family…

CHAPTER 10

Michael—Why is he

not talking to me?

—∽∿∽—

CINDY AND I HAD A long drive from New Jersey and I was tired as hell, to say the least. I had no idea that I was even moving to Virginia until Cindy picked me up from Newark International Airport, helped place my luggage in the car, and headed straight for Interstate 95.

Wait…If I remember correctly, she did allow me to say hi and good-bye to my family in Montclair, New Jersey. But after that, we were back on the road.

We arrived at her apartment in Virginia sometime around 3:00 a.m. I remember looking at her well-manicured town house and thanking God that she didn't live in a bad neighborhood (not that I couldn't adapt, but thank God there's a God). I put my bags in the closest corner I could find and went straight to bed. Cindy and I took a quick nap, woke up around 6:00 a.m., and went to gather the kids at 6:30 a.m.

Imani, Nia, and DJ were staying at Cindy's ex-husband's house for the weekend. I wasn't sure how I felt about going to pick up her kids at her ex-husband's house. I figured it was way too early in the morning for drama…and hoping her ex-husband wasn't the type.

When we arrived at the house I was greeted by the smiley face of a cheerful nine-year-old, brown-skinned girl named Nia. I was utterly amazed, if not shocked, that any kid could be so happy and excited at 6:30 a.m. on a school day. Once I made it past Lil Ms. Sunshine, I walked in the house and saw Imani getting her little brother DJ dressed for school. I was genuinely impressed by how casually Imani was getting her brother's clothes on and making sure he had all his school supplies together—after all, Imani had to be eleven years old at the time. Before I could really say hello to anybody, Cindy's ex-husband introduced himself, and we shook hands. He seemed like an all-right dude on the surface, but we'll talk about that later.

For now, I was glad that there wasn't any "baby daddy drama" going on because I know how these situations can turn completely loathsome. Meanwhile, Imani finished getting DJ dressed, and she very shyly introduced herself—the total opposite of her hyper active little sister, Nia.

Then there was DJ…

The young, handsome little four-year-old boy had the skin tone of a mini chocolate chip. DJ casually walked over to Cindy with a cool and bashful attitude.

The first thing I noticed was that DJ wasn't really into eye contact. Cool…Imani wasn't exactly giving eye contact either, and Nia was being outspoken enough for the both of them. While Nia was explaining the intricate colors of all the Power Rangers, I was taking mental notes on DJ. I noticed that DJ looked a little like Cindy's ex-husband. I also noticed Nia looked more like the ex-husband and concluded that they were both his biological kids. In retrospect, Cindy and I rarely talked about her ex-husband; I just assumed her kids were all by the same guy. In actuality, Imani had a different biological father. Anyway, Cindy never explained the kid's family dynamics, or one other important fact: that DJ had autism.

So here I am trying to break the ice with DJ and speak to him man-to-man. After all, he was Cindy's only son (…at the time) and I know how boys can be overprotective of their mothers. Since I'm a momma's boy myself, I felt it was only right that I start trying to build a relationship with Cindy's son.

First, I anxiously extended my arm to shake DJ's little hand, and that didn't go as I expected. DJ looked at my hand the same way a landlord looks at a tenant when the rent is short. Imani finally spoke and told DJ to give me five. Cool…I figured slapping five was less informal, anyway.

Once we were in the car, I began to explain to all the kids that I was happy to meet them, and that I'd be living with them in Virginia. I was speaking to everyone, but I was mainly focusing on DJ, who wasn't paying me one invisible atom of attention.

Needless to say, I felt some type of way. I mean nothing I said fazed this kid. Finally—and I do mean finally—Imani stated that DJ doesn't talk. Since I was naïve about autism or any neurological disorder, I wasn't sure what she meant by *didn't talk*. So me being me, I thought Imani meant that DJ didn't talk to strangers. I accepted that as a personal challenge and went into my Goofy voice. I do a great Goofy impression if you're into that sorta' thing. So I'm full Disney-speed ahead trying to crack this little boy's laugh code. Imani finally smiled, Nia was in laugh frenzy, and even Cindy chuckled…but not DJ. Eventually, I just pulled out some money and tried to bribe him.

I mean something had to work. So I gave all the kids five dollars apiece. When we arrived at DJ's school, Imani took DJ inside, and that's when Cindy explained that DJ had autism. Like I stated earlier, I didn't know what autism was at the time. I had never even heard the word before. So Cindy basically explained that DJ "can't" talk. That's when it hit me: *He can't talk*. I mean, I've heard of people having mental disorders and maybe I have seen somebody with autism and didn't know what it was called. But I've never met anyone who wasn't capable of speaking. I felt so bad I almost cried. I didn't know which was worse: feeling sorry for DJ or feeling sorry for Cindy because she apparently didn't want to have this conversation until it was beyond necessary.

CHAPTER 11

Cindy—Responsibilities

I HONESTLY DON'T KNOW WHY I didn't mention DJ's autism to Michael. I guess with everything else going on it slipped my mind. It's not like I go around dwelling on DJ's condition. As far as I'm concerned, DJ is just a regular kid and I…I just didn't mention it.

It was actually funny watching Michael try to get DJ's attention. A little over the top on the goofiness, but I got to see a side of Michael I never really saw before. Come to think of it, this was the first time I'd ever seen him interact with kids, and it was a pleasant surprise.

I know a lot of guys that wouldn't care if DJ or any of my kids spoke or not.

Most guys just wanted my attention and would prefer I leave my kids on the outside looking in…

I expected much more from Michael…

Being that I was carrying this man's child, it was extremely important that Michael was at least compassionate and caring toward all my children, but especially DJ.

After we dropped the kids off at school, Michael and I headed to Walmart to get some groceries. Now, I don't know how Mr. Michael was used to shopping—maybe a few items here and there—but he seemed overwhelmed by all the groceries I placed in our shopping cart.

He kept asking me, "Who's all that for?"

I had to basically explain that I had three kids and one on the way—*this was how I shopped.*

Michael almost had a heart attack when the grocery bill came to $85.

We weren't on a cruise ship with free food anymore.

Speaking of which, I still had to get my WIC checks and send in DJ's recertification documents. Taking care of DJ requires a lot of strenuous paper work. I'm constantly filling out forms, speaking with social workers, and trying to cover my back end.

Not to mention the running around that I do on a constant basis. Being three months pregnant didn't help the situation much, either. Even with my ex-husband's so-called child support, I was always playing catch-up. At the end of the day, I had Michael living with us, but these weren't exactly his kids. The child I was having for him wasn't born yet, and I guess I didn't want him to feel obligated to take care of my responsibilities. Still, I did need him to hold up his end of the bargain and help me out around the house.

But more importantly, I wanted to know if he would be able to love and care for DJ like his own.

CHAPTER 12

Michael—Oh Crap

—⟶ɯ⟵—

I HAVE TO ADMIT: As the days went by, I became a little frustrated. I didn't expect this new "family life" to be easy. Hell, I expected it to be challenging, if not hard.

But what I didn't expect was poop on the walls.

DJ was going through his potty-training stage, and every time he went to use the bathroom he would smear his feces all over the walls and sometimes the mirror.

Even worse, DJ usually got up before all of us, so by the time I went to the bathroom, there was crusty, dried-up dookey on the walls. Cindy did her best to clean the mess up before I would see it. But I usually smelled it before I saw anything. Besides, we were a team, and if there was crap on the walls, then I needed to pitch in and help clean it up.

Still and all, I wanted to figure out a way to keep DJ from spray-painting the walls with his brown graffiti. I looked on the Internet for solutions, and it was giving the typical answers: Keep a closer look on your ASD child, watch their eating habits, put them in a specialized jump suit, yadda yadda yadda…

In other words, they didn't know shit. (pun intended).

Some would suggest making DJ go to the bathroom before he went to bed. Yep, them were the fools with no kids. Anybody with a child will tell you that making a kid go number two was like making North Korea give up their nuclear weapons… That shit ain't happening.

Thus began my phase as a very light sleeper. I used to sleep so hard that I needed my bed set on fire to wake up. Nowadays, I slept with one eye open and both nostrils on guard duty. It didn't take long to realize that DJ got up around the same time every morning. But that didn't solve the problem because DJ still wouldn't use the bathroom in front of anybody.

Even if I left the door cracked, he would sit on the toilet and peek at me from the throne. Unless I was willing to wait day and night for him to make a bowel movement, I was wasting my time (no pun intended).

My lucky break came unexpectedly.

I had overslept one morning, and when I finally got up to use the bathroom I caught DJ with a nice chunk of doo-doo smearing up the wall. I basically told him *freeze* and please step away from the wall. At this point, DJ was still pretending that he didn't understand me, and I guess I was still pretending that I wasn't scared that DJ would throw the waste in my face (pun intended).

We basically had a Mexican stand-off until I ran downstairs and got his favorite candy.

I made DJ place the feces in the toilet bowl, and I promised him that he'd get the candy as a reward. But first he had to clean up all his mess, get in the shower, and pretend this never happened. After DJ spent more than an hour wiping down the walls, getting a long, thorough bathing, and finally getting his reward, he stopped smearing the walls for a few days. I can't say it didn't happen a few times again after that, but eventually he got the point.

CHAPTER 13

Nia—My Little Brother's Gonna' Be OK

I'M SIXTEEN NOW, BUT I remember DJ having autism when I was around six years old. I didn't exactly know what autism was; I kinda' overheard Mommy telling her friend about it over the phone. Mommy was crying and I really didn't understand why. Then I began to cry because I thought being autistic meant DJ was going to die or something.

I didn't want to upset my mom anymore, so I remember asking my teacher what autism was. I think my teacher was a little surprised because most kids my age weren't talking or asking about autism.

My teacher explained it the best she could. I was mainly relieved that my little brother was going to be OK. I was just getting used to being a big sister.

Sometimes I still don't understand. DJ was doing just fine until the age of two. He was actually trying to talk and was doing normal stuff that babies do. Then he stopped responding to us and looking away from everybody. At first Mommy thought he was going deaf or having a hearing problem. Autism wasn't as easy to detect then as it is now.

I can honestly say I love my brother to death. He's still one of the sweetest and most helpful people I know. I have friends with annoying little brothers, and I'm proud to say that I don't have those problems with DJ. I still often wonder what DJ would say if he could talk, how we would bond, and where his thoughts are.

But will DJ ever be able to take care of himself?

I know one thing: If anybody picks on my little brother again, I'm going to body-slam that person to the ground. I may be little, but I'm a strong big sister—*try me*.

CHAPTER 14

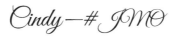

HERE'S THE THING: I KNOW DJ's situation can be a tough pill to swallow. That's why treating him like a regular kid is the best cure I can recommend for him. After all, I am extremely grateful that my son, DJ, is movie-star handsome, in physically good shape, can walk and function on his own, and doesn't need much assistance.

Simply put, his condition could be a lot worse.

People often ask me if DJ has high functioning or low functioning autism. I really don't know how to answer that. The question sounds too broad for anybody to answer. All I have to say is that DJ is functioning just fine; despite being nonverbal.

It's important that I accept the bitter with the sweet and not dwell on DJ's neurological disorder. I'd rather reward him for being a blessing. I've dedicated every fiber of my soul to making sure my children—especially DJ—have all their essentials and a few extra things. We may not be rich, but I'll be damned if we live beneath our means. My kids always have plenty of food, their own roof over their heads, a nice, safe neighborhood to live in, and stylish clothes. As long as I'm alive I will always make sure my family looks good. Why should anybody settle for less? Like I said earlier, we aren't rich, but that doesn't mean we shouldn't take pride in our appearance and well-being. I've had a few people mention how well-dressed DJ looks when he comes to school. *Well, you're damn right*...I mean, I'm not always sure if these people are being condescending or not. They almost seem surprised or something. My son always has on nice clothes and stylish sneakers. I know some parents that don't think it's necessary to buy expensive clothes for their handicapped children. As far as I'm concerned, DJ wants to look just as nice as anybody else, and I wouldn't feel right buying trendy clothes for me and my other kids, then turning around and just having DJ wearing any old tacky mess. Not on my watch...

My biggest concern is DJ being taken advantage of once I leave this earth. I kinda' wish I could live as long as DJ so I can always be there for him. And if I ever get around to building a time machine that may be realistically possible. If not, then I still want my son to have a full, wonderful life.

As much as I trust Imani, I still can't be absolutely sure if she'll take as much pride in his overall appearance the way that I do.

And as for Michael, I'm still in the process of teaching him how to dress with some style...

Ha ha, just kidding.

But seriously, I would never be able to rest in eternal peace knowing that my child wasn't looking, smelling, and feeling 100 percent fresh. Whoever thinks that's shallow either doesn't take pride in their own appearance or is too selfish to worry about their child's appearance.

No offense... Just my opinion.

CHAPTER 15

Michael—Confession

—⚭—

I KNOW A LOT OF parents wouldn't admit what I'm about to say, but I feel if I'm going to tell the story I might as well keep it real. I truly cared for Cindy, and I loved the fact that she was carrying my child, but somehow I didn't feel I was being a great role model for the kids. For starters, I didn't spend much time with them. I was more concerned with my Merchant Marine career than anything else.

It was March of 2007, and Cindy was already eight months pregnant. During this era, I wasn't taking anything too seriously except getting on a ship and sailing across seas. Meanwhile, Cindy was doing her best to help me adjust to Virginia and make us a family. In the back of my mind I knew I wanted a family, but I wasn't sure how efficient I would be as a father—especially a father to a special-needs child.

After I received my first shipping orders, I let the situation handle itself. I was off to Diego Garcia to work on a ship for four months.

That meant I wouldn't even see my son Malachi being born.

Malachi Devere Mayhew was born April 30, 2007.

When I finally saw the picture Cindy e-mailed me, I fell in love. I mean the lucky kid looked just like his daddy. For the first time ever, I felt that I was a man of substance. I had a great, adventurous job, I was sending home money to my new family, and now I had a gorgeous son that was born healthy.

I came home in July of 2007, and my dreams were as real as the photos Cindy sent me. My son Malachi looked as stunning in person as he did in the picture. I held my little man in my arms and kept kissing his face until my lips hurt. Of course I was glad to see everybody, but as you can read, my focus was more on Malachi than anything else. Which brings me to my next confession: I wasn't paying much attention to DJ at all.

I mean, I said hello…

…I said hi to everybody.

Respectfully speaking, my focus was basically on Malachi. Now, of course Cindy understood. Besides, she could command my attention whenever she wanted. And even Imani and Nia were able to talk to me here and there. As for DJ, I may have given him a high five and a quick hello, but other than that I kept my attention on Malachi.

Does that make me a bad person? Some may say yes and others may understand. Looking back, I honestly didn't mean to neglect DJ. I'm just the type of person that has a one-track mind, and when somebody doesn't literally command my attention, I will unintentionally become oblivious.

I think I found out the hard way that you shouldn't do that with a special needs child—especially DJ.

In August 2007, DJ ran away from home for the first time. I can't really say for sure if my neglect prompted DJ to leave or if he just felt like going outside for some fresh global warming air. In any case, it wasn't safe for any five-year-old child to run away.

Cindy was at a doctor's appointment with Malachi and I was at the grocery store when Imani called and asked if I took DJ with me. I told her "No," and she simply cried, "Oh my God…where is he?"

Once Imani explained that DJ was gone, I rushed back to the house and went looking for him. My younger sister was staying with us at the time, so I kinda' held her accountable. She was seventeen, and I thought I left her in charge. Normally, Imani's really good with DJ, so I figured she had everything under control, but then again, she was only eleven years old, so this whole mess really fell on my shoulders.

Call it intuition or plain old luck that I walked up the street and found DJ playing in somebody's kiddie pool. The neighbors up the block allowed DJ to play in their child's plastic pool while they waited for the police to arrive. I was so relieved that I found DJ that I was thanking the kind neighbors to death while holding DJ in my arms.

After the first squad car pulled up I began to really think about the consequences of the situation. Not only could I be arrested for child neglect, there was a good chance that DJ could be taken away from us.

Fortunately, the police reasonably understood. They didn't press any charges...they did take down my name and address.

We would be receiving a visit from Child Protective Services.

Anybody, I mean anybody that has ever had a visit from CPS will tell you that they are nerve-racking. I totally understand that CPS has to do its job—some cases are more severe than others.

However, from the moment these CPS people step inside *the home*, they treat the parents like criminals, and every child in the house becomes a potential child abuse victim.

Anyway, it was cool. At first I let Cindy deal with the female caseworker. I imagined the two black ladies would relate to each other woman-to-woman, say, "Girl, you know how it is," do the secret sista chest bump, and sing "I'm Not Gonna Cry" by Mary J. Blige.

Um, not exactly...

This CPS woman did everything but call Cindy out her name. And I wasn't too sure how much more Cindy could take. Pretty soon, the caseworker became way too overbearing and judgmental. Cindy's nostrils began to flare up, and I could tell her tongue was tired of all those self-inflicted bite marks. She was going to explode! I figured I'd intervene and avoid a war.

Once I reintroduced myself to the caseworker and explained that the incident was more my fault than Cindy's, the caseworker became a little more rational. I don't know if she appreciated my humble apology or if she was just glad to see a black father showing some concern, but strangely enough, she took a few notes and let us off with a slight verbal warning. The reason I mentioned a black father was because, to be honest, the black community really does have a bad reputation for having absentee men in the home, so I guess our home no longer fit the stereotypical profile. In any case, I liked to say we all learned our lesson and promised to keep a more watchful eye on DJ. But in the real world, things happen, and this was just the beginning.

CHAPTER 16

Cindy—Be a Father to Your Child

ON THE SURFACE, IT MAY have looked like our family was struggling. But through it all we were enjoying life and taking it all in stride. I was still in the midst of getting DJ's father to pay his child support; other than that, I didn't have too many major issues.

Michael went on another Merchant Marine assignment, and I was home taking care of the kids. I finally had a chance to spend time with my family, catch up on a few bills, and make some special treatment appointments for DJ. One of my tasks was to get him in a speech therapy class before he started kindergarten. I wasn't exactly sure how speech therapy was going to help a child that didn't talk at all, but anything was worth a shot.

Meanwhile, I spoke to DJ's father off and on and really came to the conclusion that he just wasn't trying to be a part of DJ's life.

And that hurt me to the bottom of my soul.

DJ is such a wonderful kid, and I never wanted him or Nia to experience what I went through. Truth be told, my father wasn't there for me when

I was growing up, and he died before I ever had a chance to get to really know him. I have very few memories of my father, and most of them weren't anything to brag about. I thought I avoided that mistake when I married the father of my children. It was never my intention to be somebody's "baby momma." I felt I had more to offer than that, and I needed a husband who understood the importance of his wife and children.

At the end of the day, DJ's father and I didn't work out, and he basically abandoned his children.

Even if he didn't have enough money to contribute, his moral support would have been appreciated.

But as soon as a woman—especially a black woman—takes a "dead-beat" dad to court, she gets labeled as a gold digger or lazy. Call it what you want, but there was no way in hell I was going to allow anybody to turn his back on his kids right in front of my face. So I eventually took DJ's father to court, and he subsequently had his wages garnished for lack of child-support payment. I actually felt badly about it at first. But I really think it's unforgivable to divorce your own child—especially my DJ.

CHAPTER 17

Michael—Temper Tantrums

—⁓—

LIVING LIFE OUT AT SEA definitely had its reward. Not too many jobs allow a man to travel the world for free while making money. I thought, *I could really get used to this...*but I couldn't.

I was technically a family man pretending to live a young, single bachelor's life. I justified leaving my family because I needed to make money, which was relatively true. But who was I really fooling? I enjoyed the luxury of getting away and being a part-time parent. Once I was finally honest with myself, I knew I needed to make a change.

I returned home in December of 2007. I want to say that I came home for good, but I was actually on emergency leave for my grandmother's funeral. By this time, DJ was turning six, and he was becoming a little more difficult to handle. According to Cindy, DJ had been throwing some serious temper tantrums.

In the past, DJ would have meltdowns. That's when DJ would cry uncontrollably for a few minutes and calm down on his own accord.

These tantrums we're different.

DJ would have these outrageous hissy fits whenever he couldn't get his way about something.

Cindy started recording these tantrums so she could show the doctors and specialists.

DJ had been recorded jumping up and down, screaming at the top of his lungs, kicking the walls, spinning around on the ground, and whatever else he learned in Tasmanian devil school. To top it off, if anybody interrupted his little number, he'd purposely bite them wherever his teeth could do the most damage.

In my opinion, Cindy was being a little too lenient due to DJ's autistic condition. For a parent that claimed to treat DJ like a normal child, she was letting him go way too far.

Now understand, I'm just as sympathetic to DJ's disorder as anybody else. I also held a little guilt for not being more involved in his upbringing. But now that I was back home, it was seriously time for me to become more proactive.

It was 7:00 a.m. and Cindy was desperately trying to get DJ ready for school. I had already witnessed a couple of his tantrums firsthand.

Before, I just observed and let Cindy handle it her way. This particular morning, DJ looked like he was going berserk as he banged his head up against the wall. So I sternly grabbed DJ by the arm and made him stop!

And guess what? By some strange miracle, DJ actually calmed down.

I was a little worried about what Cindy would think. She kept looking at me, then looking at DJ, and then looking back to me. But she saw for herself what a little dose of discipline could do. The stricter I became with DJ, the less tantrums he would have.

You see, there's a very big difference between child abuse and taking control of your own child. I personally feel that society knows the difference as well, but there are still some parents that would rather have our children on useless drugs than take control of the situation themselves.

Now, DJ still has meltdowns from time to time where he may cry, become depressed or even clutch his fist out of frustration. I can totally understand that... But I don't tolerate tantrums and DJ knows better. As a real father, I would rather discipline my child early than have society or these uncanny medicines do it for me.

Cindy—Commitment

HAVING MICHAEL AROUND WAS GREAT, when he was actually around. I understood that he had a career that he loved, and I met him on those terms. However, we also spoke about marriage a few times, and somehow I was doing most of the talking. Things really became complicated when I let him know that I was pregnant again...

When I told Michael I was pregnant with our first child, he was kinda' shocked, but he wasn't disappointed. This time seemed different. I really don't think he was anticipating another child. As for me, I was ecstatic. I loved this man, and I loved the family we were building; now more than ever, I needed him to be on the same page.

While I was pregnant, everybody pitched in to help me adjust. Imani already knew the routine, and Nia was now old enough to help as well. Basically, I needed help tending to Malachi and DJ, grocery shopping, preparing our meals, and cleaning up around the house. That's when I discovered that my little DJ doesn't mind housework.

I'm not exactly sure who taught DJ how to use a vacuum, but the kid was a natural. I guess I underestimated how brilliant DJ can be at certain things. I mean, he was only six years old, and he held the vacuum like a professional cleaner. Please understand, regular chores and vacuuming may seem like a small indication of responsibility for the average child, but for DJ this was a milestone. For the first time, I watched my son take pride in doing something. DJ wasn't just going through the motions or mimicking somebody else's behavior; he really seemed like he knew that it was his responsibility to vacuum and help clean.

Meanwhile, Michael was away on another assignment. This time he was stationed in Saipan, wherever the hell that is. He would call maybe two or three times a week—not as often as I needed him to call.

So much was happening with DJ that I wanted Michael to be home and share this experience with us. I finally had DJ in another speech therapy class, where his teachers were attempting to teach him sign language. To this day, DJ can use a little bit of the sign language they taught him, just not enough to communicate on a daily basis. I wasn't sure what it would take to get DJ to talk, and I'm still committed to trying every angle and leaving no stone unturned.

I really needed help raising DJ, dealing with my pregnancy mood swings, and just having a companion in general. These were some of the saddest times I can recall.

By the time Michael returned from overseas, I was seven months pregnant. Time was flying by—with or without the fun. My children kept me entertained most of the time, but I missed having Michael around as my partner. I don't think Michael was home for a week before he was talking about taking another assignment. This time, he was leaving to work in Japan for six months. Enough was enough. Like I stated earlier, I knew that he had to focus on his career. I also needed him to be committed to his family.

Before Mr. Bon Voyage left on his next assignment, I decided to have my labor induced. He hadn't been there to see Malachi born—I was determined for him to be in the delivery room for our newest addition to the family.

Malik Devere Mayhew was born September 27, 2008.

I watched Michael gently take Malik in his arms like he was the genesis of a new world.

I guess I was worried for nothing.

Actually, one thing still concerned me: Once again, I was a single mother, and I had two of my latest children with a man who didn't seem interested in marriage. Also, he was leaving the very next day for Japan. I don't think I was asking for much; I just needed to know that our relationship wasn't only about making kids.

CHAPTER 19

Michael—I Was Afraid

—⚡—

WHAT CAN I SAY?

I guess I was born selfish.

I'd spent my entire life trying to find a career like the Merchant Marines, and I refused to let it go. Not even my army career was as rewarding as my ship life.

But things were different now.

I basically had five children—one of them a special needs child—and a girlfriend that wanted me to seal the deal with a marriage certificate.

Keep in mind that all of this happened in less than two years.

Lord Jesus, help me…

Sure, I could give up my shipping life and stay at home with the family. Can somebody tell me how I was ever going to make the money I was making on the ships back home? I was thirty-four years old with no college education or any other training except the military. Not to mention the fact that I loved to travel.

I personally felt that Cindy should be happy that I was sending money home.

As a matter of fact, I once challenged *her* to get an awesome paying job and to let me sit at home with the kids. Of course, she just brushed me off with the flick of her right hand.

So...

Here I am in Japan on another shipping assignment, and all I can think about is my family falling apart. I knew I needed to be at home raising my sons, and DJ was becoming the biggest factor.

Not only was DJ finally developing more mental capabilities; he was showing genuine signs of growth and maturity. This was the time that I should be outside in the backyard throwing him the football or somewhere teaching him how fish. OK, I don't know how to fish, but we could be learning together.

One might ask: If you know all this, then why were you still shipping?

Because...I was afraid.

I was simply afraid that all I had to offer this family was the money I was sending home. I was afraid that if DJ wasn't developing fast enough, that I failed as a parent. I was afraid that Cindy could be doing much better, and I was standing in her way. I was afraid that once I stayed still long enough, everyone could see how afraid I really was.

I've never been responsible for anybody but myself. Then, in what seemed like an overnight big bang theory, I was an instant father and the chosen pioneer for the family I helped create.

I dunno, I just felt that Cindy was doing fine before she met me, and I just complicated things.

To make matters worse, I was letting my worries affect my job performance. I wasn't taking pride in my duties because it all felt like a waste of time.

I was needed back home.

I finally gave up my shipping career and returned home in December of 2008. I didn't know how I was going to survive, but I decided my family was worth the effort.

CHAPTER 20

Cindy—Alarms on the Doors

IN THE SUMMER OF 2008, our family moved to Concord, North Carolina. I had my fair share of fun in Virginia, and now I needed to move on. It was time to compromise with Michael so he could be closer to his family, especially his mother in Statesville, North Carolina.

I found a cook job at Olive Garden, while Michael enrolled in a community college in Charlotte.

I don't think the kids cared for North Carolina at first; after all, what kid wants to leave their old friends behind and start from scratch? Mainly Imani and Nia were complaining; the boys were too young to really care.

I think DJ may have been excited about his new environment—maybe a little too excited.

For the second time, DJ went missing.

This time, I was at home when it happened. It was early in the morning, and something told me to wake up and check on the kids. Sure enough, DJ wasn't in the house.

52

I wasn't sure how long he was gone, but I immediately called the police while Michael and Imani went to look for him. When the police showed up, I gave a description of DJ, and they alerted all the other units in the vicinity. About twenty minutes later, a squad car pulled up with DJ in the back seat. I was extremely embarrassed that this happened, and even more embarrassed that DJ snuck out the house without wearing any shoes or a shirt. At least he was smart enough to put on a pair of pants.

Based on DJ's obvious condition, the police officers understood and almost seemed sympathetic. They informed us of an Alzheimer patient that did the same thing a few months ago and suggested that we get alarms for our doors. I don't know why I didn't think about that before, but I sure did rush up to Walmart and get an alarm for the front and the back doors.

CHAPTER 21

Imani—Doing our best

☙

OMG! I MEAN SERIOUSLY, I was so worried that DJ wasn't going to be found. I never thought in a million years that he'd actually sneak out the house while we were all asleep. I'm surprised I didn't hear him.

It's bad enough that he's sneaking out at the age of six, but this little boy doesn't even get dressed when he goes trotting off. That's bad because there are a lot of creeps in this world, and anything could have happened to DJ. On the other hand, the reason the cops spotted DJ so fast was because he *was* the only little boy in town walking around half naked. So at least they were able to find him quickly.

We were all upset for the rest of the day. The only thing Mommy could think about was securing the house so that this wouldn't happen again.

It's crazy because when we were living in Virginia, he only pulled this stunt that one time when we weren't paying close enough attention to him. But now I noticed that DJ kept trying to roam around every time we went outside.

The last thing we needed were those CPS people coming around and interrogating us again. Trust me, DJ comes from a loving home, and we're all doing our best to make sure that he's safe and well protected. It's just that DJ's so quiet that it's hard to keep up with him without watching his every single move.

CHAPTER 22

Michael—I Dunno...

—ᴍ—

THIS WAS EXACTLY WHAT I was afraid of...

When DJ snuck out the house, I felt like I let the family down again. Yeah, it happened while we were all in the house asleep, but as a protector of the home, I felt I should have prevented this from happening.

Now, I had to figure out how to keep DJ from running outside. It's not like I could ask DJ why he wants to go outside. Where is he trying to hang out? Or what's the reason for it all?

Realistically, most six-year-old boys just want to hang out and play *Tom Sawyer*. However, most six-year-olds also understand that they could get in trouble with their parents for sneaking out the house. In DJ's case, I can't enforce any consequences, because I honestly don't think he understands that he's doing anything wrong by leaving the house.

I dunno...

Like I said, I'm not an expert on this type of thing. But I wasn't about to make matters worse by reprimanding him for something that I could help him avoid.

Not only did we get alarms on the doors, I spent many late nights on the couch in the living room, securing the front door.

CHAPTER 23

Cindy—Family

BESIDES SNEAKING OUT OF THE house, DJ wasn't really giving us any hard-core trouble. After all, he'd stopped smearing crap on the walls, chewing the upper part of his shirt (whatever that was about), peeing in the bed, and crying for no reason. He had also come a long way from his temper tantrum phase. Of course, DJ was still sneaking snacks in his room, using too much salt, and overdosing on Reese's Peanut Butter Cups. Overall, I felt he was showing a lot of progress. We were all working as a family to give DJ a stable home and unconditional love—that's the best we could do.

It's really about the family sticking together. And not just our immediate family: DJ has a long list of relatives who really care about him.

For instance, my younger sister Tonya, always asks about DJ and would send him things whenever she could. Tonya is one of DJ's closest aunts and practically a part of our immediate family.

DJ also has his Uncle Ryan, two aunts on Michael's side of the family named Yennoco and Yoomi, his

Aunt Mellisa in New Jersey, a wonderful and caring grandfather (Michael's father, O'Conney), and three grandmothers: Michael's step-mother, Alfretta; my mother, Noreen; and Michael's mother, Pam.

Pam or, as I call her, Pammy Whammy, loves her some DJ. The moment I met Pam, she gave us all a hug, but when she hugged DJ, she almost wouldn't let him go. I had assumed Michael already explained DJ's autism to Pam because she never asked me anything about it. All Pammy seemed to care about were the grandkids she always wanted.

I knew Mike was really close with his mother; that's why I didn't mind moving closer to her in North Carolina. And it was well worth it. She always invited us to her home, and her fried chicken is the bomb.

DJ is very particular about food and would rather eat a Reese's Peanut Butter Cup before he eats a real meal. But when it came to Grandma Pam's chicken, he didn't mind eating one, two, maybe five drumsticks before we had to tell DJ, *enough...*

I really like when we get together and have family cookouts. I think those are the moments that DJ is most relaxed and cheerful.

Usually, Tonya is either playing with DJ or showing him something on her cell phone. Or my mother, Noreen, is teaching DJ how to prepare one of her special Caribbean dishes. I wish we could have cookouts all year round. There's something about being outdoors, and grilling some good food that puts us all in a great mood.

CHAPTER 24

Michael—Grandma Pam

—⚋—

MY MOTHER HAS ALWAYS PLAYED a very instrumental part of my life. She's helped me make wise decisions that have kept me alive to this day. That's why I remember so vividly the day I told her that she was going to become a grandmother. I called my mother from Hawaii while I was still on the ship with Cindy. I basically explained to my mother that I met a girl named Cindy, and she was pregnant with my child. So naturally, my mother knew she was about to become somebody's grandma. What she didn't know was that I was coming to her house with three other children. I always like to surprise my mother. Her reactions be priceless…

When we arrived at Pam's apartment in Statesville, I allowed Cindy to walk through the door first, and then one by one, my mother hugged and kissed everybody. And without really knowing DJ, she hugged him harder than anyone. I guess because DJ tried to sneak past Pam without giving her "sum sugar" is why he became her main focus. I'm just guessing, I don't really know. I do know that before we left that evening, I explained to her that DJ had autism and that's why he wasn't always being responsive. My mother never questioned me about it, and it never became the topic of conversation. DJ was now her grandchild; that's all that mattered.

On another note, my mother was concerned about my relationship with Cindy. Even before my youngest son, Malik, was born, my mother would often ask me when I planned to marry Cindy. I really didn't have an answer for her, which was the wrong answer.

My mother simply explained that Cindy seemed like a nice young lady, and since I seemed to love her enough to have children with her, I might as well marry her. After all, time waits for no man. *True...*

I mean, it's not that I didn't want to marry Cindy or have her in my life forever; I just figured I'd finish my career and...

"Boy, stop making excuses, before you become an excuse," my mother said.

Cindy and I decided to get married on July 30' 2011. We had a beautiful ceremony with all our kids and other family members.

DJ was our ring bearer.

Cindy's mother helped cater the wedding reception, and I pretty much danced the night away. I managed to sneak in a dance with DJ when the DJ (um... Disk Jockey), played the song, "Go DJ," by Lil Wayne. I had to practically fight Tonya for DJ so I could dance with him. She had been hogging the boy all night. In my mind, that was the song I personally chose for DJ, so I really needed him on the dance floor.

Pam couldn't have been happier. She finally lived to see the day that I had a wife and kids and became the man she raised me to be.

As the years went by, I would visit my mother in Statesville and usually take DJ with me. Even if the rest of the family was still sleep or busy, I always managed to bring DJ.

And that really meant a lot to her.

On August 16, 2014, my mother Pam had an aneurism that left her partially brain-dead. She survived the stroke, but she still isn't able to speak or walk. During this dark chapter of my life, I needed my family the most. I kept going over all the things my mother tried to explain to me when she was able to talk. And it all finally made sense.

During one of her hospital visits, I watched DJ place his hand over Grandma Pam's head. I guess he realized she wasn't feeling well and wanted to take her temperature. I swear on everything, I would love to know what DJ was thinking at that moment. I can't say if my mother will ever fully recover, and I often pray that she does. But I can now truly emphasize with Cindy because I live for the day my special loved one will be able to talk again.

CHAPTER 25

TONYA—THRILLS

⌒

YES, I'M AUNTIE TONYA, AND I'm definitely a part of this immediate family. Cindy's my big sister, and she practically helped raise me when we were living in Brooklyn. So of course I remember when she had Imani and I soon became Imani's babysitter.

I was really close with Imani before Cindy moved to Virginia to be with what's-his-name. By the time I moved to Virginia, I had two more relatives: Nia and DJ. Of course I loved them as well, and I helped take care of them the same way I did for Imani.

I love all my nieces and nephews for different reasons. I'm fond of Imani because she reminds me of myself when I was her age, not to mention she was the first daughter I never had. Then I could never get over Nia's crazy tales. I still remember Nia pulling off her diaper and waving it in the air like she just don't care. And of course DJ was my first nephew, and I've always been extremely fond of him.

I think it's a wonderful challenge to get DJ's undivided attention.

Most kids do stupid stuff to get grown-ups' attention, but with DJ, you have to earn his attention. He don't pay attention to just anybody. I feel DJ was a blessing from God, and it goes to show you that God don't make mistakes.

We don't cry or feel sorry for DJ over here...

We know his potential, and we strive to make sure that he has a happy and fulfilling life. Now, these lil brats that Cindy had with Mike are a mess...I can deal with Malachi because he's a sweet little boy when it's just him and me, one-on-one. But when Malachi hooks up with Malik, they are a handful of trouble. It's funny because DJ is twelve years old, Malachi is eight, and Malik is only six. But somehow Malik acts like he's the big little brother. It happens, I guess. I just get a thrill out of watching all of them.

Now, one thrill I didn't enjoy was when DJ snuck out the house *on me.* Yes, I was there. Keep in mind, I've heard about DJ doing this, and I was saying to myself, *How do they keep letting this happen?* But I will admit firsthand that DJ moves like an invisible panther.

We were all in the living room watching TV when Mike came in the room and asked, "Where's DJ?" I started to look around the house, but Mike ran out the door like the house was on fire.

That's when my heart jumped and I ran outside behind him.

No shoes or nothing...I just ran!

So we hopped in Mike's car and started speeding down the street. We circled the block a few times, and we were just about to give up and call the police.

The next thing I knew, Mike said, "There he is."

And sure enough, DJ was rushing up the street wearing nothing but a pair of boxer shorts. When I tell you I was pissed…I was pissed. I guess I was mad at DJ for sneaking out of the house, but I was also upset with myself for not paying attention when he walked out. The moral of the story is that it's easy to judge other people when you haven't walked a mile in their shoes. I may be Auntie Tonya, but I'm not the one that's putting in work 365 days out of the year. I feel that Mike and Cindy are doing a great job raising DJ and all their children. I applaud them for being so strong. Because I almost had a heart attack and I was only there for the weekend.

CHAPTER 26

Cindy—God's Grace

WELL, ONE THING I CAN say…

…there aren't too many dull moments in our household.

By the grace of God, DJ stopped running away in December 2010, when we moved to our new town house complex. I don't know if it was the change of scenery, or if DJ just stopped running away on his own accord. Either way, DJ hasn't run away since he was seven years old. That was our biggest challenge to date, and we were able to get through it as a family.

Those were some of the scariest moments of my life, and I don't know what I would have done on my own. There are so many things that can go wrong with DJ, that I'm constantly on my toes trying to avoid the worst-case scenarios.

The struggle is never over.

DJ could decide to run away tomorrow, and we'd be at square one. All I can do at this point is pray that DJ and our family overcome each challenge and learn from the experience.

CHAPTER 27

Cindy—Curriculum

HAVING FIVE CHILDREN WOULD BE a challenge for almost anybody. And raising a special-needs child makes things more challenging.

Since the day I found out that DJ was diagnosed with autism, I've made it my personal mission to make DJ's life as wonderful as possible.

Once I stopped looking for some miraculous cure, I understood that DJ was fine just the way he is. And let's be real, I've seen children that weren't diagnosed with anything, and they seem to give their parents more trouble than DJ has ever given me.

And that speaks volumes.

Still and all, I have always tried to be a concerned parent, and my top priority was to enroll DJ in the best schools possible. All my children deserve a well-rounded education. With DJ, it's more than essential that he's in a learning environment where he's comfortable with the teachers, staff, and other classmates. I moved to Concord because I did some research on the school systems and was pleased with the positive reviews. Overall, the

Concord schools had more advanced programs for special-needs students.

When I enrolled DJ into middle school, I personally spoke to each teacher one on one and made a list of all of DJ's behavioral, eating, and sleeping habits. Also, I wanted to know the other teachers' credentials and how long they had been teaching professionally. I know it seems a little over the top. But I needed DJ to obtain a broad range of curriculum skills that I wasn't able to teach him at home. Otherwise, DJ would be in a class being babysat, and not really learning anything.

Most of DJ's teachers were excellent. Mr. Lafave was DJ's teacher from third to fourth grade, and he worked miracles with DJ's capabilities. Under Mr. Lafave's watch, DJ learned more sign language, computer skills, proper eating etiquette, and a wonderful list of other necessary skills. When I saw my baby write his name for the first time, I had to hold my heart to keep from dropping dead.

Although DJ still has difficulty speaking or learning any basic academic skills like math and English, his socialization skills went from zero to one hundred real quick.

I would visit DJ's school every chance I could get so I could watch him interact with his fellow classmates. I'll admit that I was still a little upset that DJ was the only autistic student in his class that was unable to speak. I was hoping he'd have at least one nonverbal classmate that he could advance in speech therapy with. In any case, Mr. Lafave worked with DJ one-on-one with his speech therapy, and I was overjoyed with DJ's curriculum goals.

CHAPTER 28

Cindy—Are You Serious?

OF COURSE, WITH THE GOOD comes the evil, and I touch on this subject with a heavy heart. I appreciate all the teachers that were and still are a part of DJ's educational process; unfortunately, one of DJ's instructors seriously crossed the line.

On October 7, 2014, I received a phone call from a concerned teacher that DJ was being "mistreated." Apparently, the teacher who called me had witnessed another teacher putting hot sauce on DJ's finger so that DJ wouldn't pick his nose.

Are you freaking serious!? I almost couldn't believe what I was hearing.

Let me get this straight…

Some teacher allegedly put hot sauce on DJ's finger because she couldn't get my eleven-year-old son with special needs to stop picking his nose?

I immediately called the principal so I could get to the bottom of this.

By the time I spoke to the principal, the whole incident was brushed off as a rumor, and the teacher in question had been suspended.

That raised my eyebrows to the ceiling. In my mind, I wondered why the principal would suspend a teacher if the rumor wasn't true.

Only a real parent would understand what I did next. I marched my ass up to DJ's school so I could speak with the principal face-to-face. That's when I was greeted with misinformation and a bunch of damage-control techniques. Basically, the principal stated that her hands were tied and the case was being handled by the Board of Education. Keep in mind, the principal never denied the accusation; she merely told me that the teacher had been suspended and that the situation was going through the chain of custody.

That's it, I thought, *I'm going to the police.*

I couldn't think of any logical reason that this teacher wasn't in jail or at least being questioned by the local authorities.

Then, I finally got a taste of reality and how things work.

When I first went to the police, I spoke with a detective that specializes in child abuse cases. I was almost relieved when the detective expressed his concern for DJ and promised he'd get me some vital answers about the case. After a week of waiting for a response, I called the detective back, hoping he'd have something to tell me.

And to my utter disappointment, the detective told me there was nothing he could do; the Board of Education was handling the case.

I nearly lost my mind. I couldn't believe that the Board of Education had so much power. I could understand if this was an administrative problem or curriculum issue, but this was flat-out child abuse.

This so-called instructor took it upon herself to use an unorthodox technique to discipline my son. Not to mention, DJ has autism and can't speak. There's no telling how long this has been going on or what else this person did to my son.

The detective didn't seem to care anymore. He simply explained that once the Board of Education gets involved, the ball is in their court.

So, I just marched down to one of the Board of Education meetings to get some answers.

At this point, I know I'm getting the runaround. I mean it's been a week since the incident was reported at the school, and nobody—I mean nobody—had bothered to contact me. You would think that they could at least tell me their version of what happened to DJ and explain why they suspended the alleged culprit.

When I attended the Board of Education meeting I was angry, nervous, uncomfortably anxious, and ready to take on *the machine.* I had had enough of these people giving me the runaround, and I deserved the respect all parents would want if they were in my shoes.

And even as a concerned parent, I still wasn't allowed to speak at the open forum meeting.

According to the Board of Education, I had to give them prior notice of the incident, and then have it addressed at the next meeting.

And that's how they play...

The members of the Board of Education use their own laws and protocols to the best of their advantage. There wasn't one reason why I shouldn't have been granted an immediate hearing or at least get a few answers about what happened to my son.

What?

Am I supposed to get my son's version?

DJ can't talk, for God's sake!

I honestly couldn't believe that something like this could happen. And they wouldn't make an exception due to the circumstances?

I could only think of one other thing.

I called the news station.

There was no way in hell that all these people were going to pretend that nothing happened to DJ. I wouldn't hear of it.

Channel 9 News was more than happy to address the issue. Of course they did their own background investigation to make sure it was a legitimate story. And sure enough, they wanted to interview us two days later.

Anybody interested in viewing the news clip can look it up on YouTube at https://youtu.be/JmFQrNPzMak ("Teacher accused of using hot sauce to discipline student").

After this nightmare, I was reluctant to send DJ back to school. I had to convince myself that this was an isolated incident and it would never happen again.

All I can do is pray that it doesn't.

It's not fair! DJ has special needs, and I truly feel that his rights have been violated on all levels.

This time, it's not just about DJ or autism in general; it's about every parent's worst fear: child abuse. What happened to DJ could easily happen to any child. Hopefully, most children will be able to speak and give their side of the story.

Then again, will anybody care?

CHAPTER 29

Michael—Abuse of Power

—◇◇◇—

"SHE DID WHAT!?" I ASKED Cindy, puzzled.

I quickly pulled my car over on the shoulder of Interstate 77 and put the phone close to my ear. I couldn't believe what Cindy was telling me.

Somebody at DJ's school had put hot sauce on his finger?

WTF!?

Why?

Once I got all the details I still didn't get it. I refused to believe that this so-called teacher was simply trying to get DJ to stop "picking his nose."

I honestly felt that only a sadistic control freak with the human spirit of the devil would be capable of such an act of cruelty.

This is DJ...

...*my* DJ.

He wasn't some undisciplined dog that needed corrective training. What happened to DJ shouldn't even happen to a dog. What if DJ was allergic to hot sauce or just died of complications due to hot pepper sauce going up his nose?

This was a total outrage.

When I went home, I had to console Cindy for over an hour. I've never seen this strong, black woman break down and cry so hard in all the years I've known her.

Our entire family was at a loss. Nobody could believe that this was happening. Even worse, nothing could be done about it.

The teacher that allegedly put the hot sauce on DJ's finger wasn't really "suspended." It was more like transferred. We were informed that she had another teaching job at a different school. Of course, that only added salt to injury.

It was a painful mess.

This may come out wrong, but I wanted to slap the piss out this teacher…or better yet, to put some hot sauce on her child's finger and watch it go up his or her nostrils.

Damn, I take that back.

Even though this teacher may have abused my child, I would never want it to happen to another child.

So please forgive me for my anger.

I just can't figure out who is to blame: the teacher that committed the act of abuse or the Board of Education that systematically covers everything up? They both demonstrate an abuse of power.

When I looked for similar stories on YouTube I was disgusted by how many times this has happened across the country.

Then it all made sense.

As long as the Board of Education can avoid lawsuits, they can easily transfer unethical teachers from school to school to cover their asses.

Every day I pray for my kids...
    ...all my kids.
    Because I feel this country is capable of anything.

CHAPTER 30

Imani—Strength

❧

I SAT DOWN ON THE floor, leaned my back against Mommy's closed bedroom door, and quietly listened to her cry and sob. From experience, I knew better than to bother her when she was this upset. Besides, Michael was in the room with her, so hopefully he could calm her down.

Then again, he seemed so frustrated and angry that they both might need a chill pill before they lose their minds.

There are so many emotions floating around in my head. I don't know which one to grasp and let take control.

I guess anger comes to mind.

But my heart is telling me forgiveness.

The teacher who abused DJ probably didn't know any better. Maybe that's how she was raised, or hot sauce is a part of her culture. Who knows?

I know this isn't the first time somebody has taken advantage of DJ, and unfortunately, it probably won't be the last. I don't know how broad the entire autism spectrum is, or if there are a million unknown traits. I do know that DJ has a particular disorder that makes him the sweetest, most gentle creature on earth. And that's not good in the type of world we live in. I often wonder if my baby bro is an angel pretending to be handicapped. Why else would God make somebody so pure and innocent and leave him in this hellhole? The worst thing I've ever seen DJ do was eat too many Reese's Peanut Butter Cups. And if that's a sin, then hell must look like Willy Wonka's Chocolate Factory.

All jokes aside, I don't know if I'll ever have the courage to have kids. I've watched my mother raise us, and it took all the strength she has just to make it to her job and provide for us. I don't feel I'm strong enough for that. I guess that's why the heart is technically the strongest muscle in your body.

One day, I'll be an obstetrician, and it will be my responsibility to bring children into the world. I'm still trying to imagine how I'm going to tell an anxious parent that their child is one out of the sixty-eight children who are diagnosed with autism every year. Hopefully, they'll understand and be as strong as my mom. Because if that child is anything like DJ, they should see that the glass is half full.

CHAPTER 31

DJ—MY TIME LINE

◆ ◆ ◆

Newborn

* I was born Sunday morning, December 29, 2002.
* I went to my new home Tuesday, Dec. 31.
* I met my sisters, Imani and Nia.
* I celebrated my first New Year's Day. (That was quick!)
* I met Grandma Noreen, Aunt Tonya, and Uncle Ryan.

Age 1

* I was christened at a local church in Norfolk, Virginia.
* I took my first steps.
* I tasted a Reese's Peanut Butter Cup for the first time. (Yummy!!!)
* I said my first words, like *ma-ma*, *da-da*, and *no*.

Age 2

* Mommy braided my hair (ouch!).
* I started day care.
* I was diagnosed with nonverbal autism.
* I went to lots of doctor's appointments. (Too many doctors poked and touched me.)

Age 3

* Mommy got me a Spiderman cake for my birthday
* I got my first haircut (ouch!).
* I got really sick from eating too many Reese's Peanut Butter Cups.
* I went right back to eating more Reese's Peanut Butter Cups. (You can't deny the taste!)
* I went to the dentist for the first time. I learned to say, "*Ah…*"
* I had my front teeth pulled. (No more "*ah*" for you, Buddy.)

Age 4

* I started special-needs classes at a new day care center.
* Mommy hugged me good-bye for a long time.
* I jumped in the pool like a big boy. (Seven feet! Cow-a-bunga!)

- Big Sister Imani came to help me play in the water.
- I went to my first movie theater with Big Sister Nia.
- Mommy came home!
- I met Michael. (I guess he's OK.)
- I learned how to potty train (and draw on the wall).
- Michael went bye-bye.

Age 5

- No more diapers.
- My front teeth started to grow back.
- I got a new baby brother named Malachi.
- Michael came home.
- I went outside by myself for the first time.
- Michael found me at my new pool.
- A caseworker tried to ask me questions, but I can't speak...talk to the hand!
- I started Kindergarten.
- Michael went bye bye.
- I began throwing tantrums.
- Michael came home.
- Never mind, no more tantrums.
- Mommy took me to Kings Dominion amusement park. (I rode my first roller coaster. Awesome!)
- Michael went bye-bye.
- I learned a little sign language.

- I helped Mommy by learning how to vacuum.
- Michael came home.
- I got a new baby brother named Malik.
- Michael went bye-bye.
- I Was Dracula for Halloween.

Age 6

- I wore my first pair of Nike Jordans. (Yeah, I'm cool!)
- Michael came home.
- I spent my first birthday with Michael home.
- I went to Chuck E. Cheese's for the first time.
- I moved to Concord, North Carolina.
- I started first grade.
- I went outside by myself again. (I came home in a police car.)
- I began to take my clothes off in front of company. (I'm a young Chippendale!)

Age 7

- I went outside by myself. (It was really cold outside!)
- I moved to a new town house.
- No more running away.
- I started second grade.
- I went to New Jersey to visit my family (a very long drive).

❀ I saw New York City for the first time—so many buildings, lights, and good hot dogs!

Age 8

❀ I had to repeat second grade. (*Aw, man!*)
❀ I rode the school bus by myself. (I mean, other kids were on the bus, but Mommy and Daddy didn't drop me off.)
❀ I met my favorite teacher. Mr. Lafave.
❀ I learned how to interact with my classmates.
❀ I made a good friend named Adam.
❀ I learned how to spell my name: I'm Desmond Joseph, a.k.a. DJ.
❀ I went to the YMCA, the zoo, an amusement park, and a museum all in one year!
❀ I tried to ride a roller coaster again. (Get me *off* this thing!)

Age 9

❀ I went to my first Autism Walk and had a blast!
❀ I laughed at Mommy and Michael. They couldn't keep up with Malik and me.
❀ My teachers at school want me to start another speech therapy class.
❀ Mr Lafave taught me more computer skills.
❀ I had to bite Malik to let him know who's in charge.

❧ I love my little brothers.

Age 10

❧ I started third grade. (Yay!)
❧ Mr Lafave was no longer my teacher. (No!)
❧ I still have my friend Adam. (Life goes on.)
❧ I went to the Special Olympics and won lots of medals in track and field.
❧ I went to my second Autism Walk. (Mommy and Michael finally kept up this time.)
❧ Nia taught me how to do the "cha-cha slide dance." I still don't know why.
❧ I went to Florida to visit Aunt Tonya. (The heat made me hot and sticky. Yuck!)

Age 11

❧ I went to visit Grandma Pam in the hospital.
❧ I started fourth grade.
❧ I learned a little sign language and was awarded Most Helpful Student in Class.
❧ I started folding my own clothes—and even Nia's clothes—when she was being lazy.
❧ I saw my first 3-D movie. (I don't like wearing the 3-D glasses, but I love the popcorn!)

Age 12

❧ I started fifth grade.

- I went trick-or-treating with Malachi and Malik, but I didn't feel like wearing a costume…I'm grown!
- I went to Virgina to visit Grandma Noreen for a family cookout.
- I graduated from fifth grade with flying colors!
- My school sent home a communication device called Dynavox. (Cool!)
- Mommy and Michael came up with this crazy idea to write a book about me called *That's My DJ*…it better be good!

CHAPTER 32

Cindy—Autism Moms Rock

THERE HAVE BEEN A FEW dark chapters in our book, and sometimes our day-to-day events have been one unpredictable page after the next. Through it all, we know we have one another, so our world goes on as usual. Most of the negative trials and tribulations that took place on our journey were helpful warnings that provided our family with infinite wisdom.

When I gave birth to DJ, I thought that I had it all figured out. I had no idea that I would have a son with autism that would ultimately test my skills as a parent and shape me into a more caring and loving person.

I can't imagine DJ being raised by anybody else.

Nobody on this earth can love DJ the way that I do, and I get the honor of being his mother for the rest of my life.

Every day I watch my son do amazing things that other parents might take for granted.

Before DJ turned two years old, he took his first step. I was excited. It was cute. But I'd seen that before. Imani did the same thing years ago, and so did Nia. After DJ was diagnosed with autism, it seemed everything DJ did had become a miracle. Simply brushing his teeth every day is worth getting up early to watch.

As DJ moves forward in life, I get to wonder what beautiful thing he'll do next for Mommy. Will he draw me another beautiful picture of purple flowers that look like his crayon pollinated a new breed of daisy-roses? When he finishes eating, will he remember to take his plate to the sink and wash his own dish?

Can I get a hug without asking?

Oh my God, will I hear DJ's voice for the very first time?

Does DJ have a deep, smooth, melodic voice, or is it high-pitched and mellow? How many words has he accumulated that are waiting to bust out of those strong vocal chords of his?

These are the things that my dreams are made of.

Yes, I love all my children to death.

Imani is nineteen and has become one of my best friends (when we're not annoying each other). As bad as Nia is, I still love getting her hair braided and watching Ms. Thang walk around the house like she's the cutest thing since ice cream was invented. Malachi knows so much about dinosaurs that I need to enroll him in a school for paleontologists so *he* can teach *them* how to discover new breeds of fossils. And Malik, of course, is Mommy's football star.

Then there's DJ…
DJ, DJ…DJ!
Desmond Joseph has been on this earth for twelve amazing years, and there hasn't been a day that goes by that I don't thank God for my miracle child. (Not to sound too sappy and sentimental.) Only a mother with an autistic child can understand what I go through for my children.

Autism moms Rock!

The next time you hold your children, look in their eyes and be thankful that they stare back at you. Even if they are acting like they're too grown up, or too cute to be loved by their old, corny parents, it's still a blessing.

I may not be able to hear DJ's voice.

That's OK for now…

…those big, mahogany eyes say it all.

I love you, DJ.

Mommy

CHAPTER 33

Michael—Sonlight

—◊—

FROM THE MOMENT YOU ENTERED my life...I was blessed with a sight.

You became my guiding light...

That made my future bright.

You've never said a word, and I have yet to hear you speak, but I listen to your heart, and with each beat you tell a speech.

The world may not understand... who cares about this world?

We have vision on our side, and that's a diamond with a pearl.

Can I have your attention, or will you please accept mine?

Just to see you smile leaves me frozen in time.

They say you are a puzzle, but all I see is one piece. You were made in God's image, and the picture is unique.

I don't know much about autism...

...nobody does.

I'll assume it's just a word for unconditional love...

Yesterday I saw a dove, and those feathers were so bright. When you entered my life, you became my *son*light.

Love,

Dad

Frequently Asked Questions (FAQ)

▲ ▲ ▲

1) What was the inspiration for *THAT'S MY DJ*?

Cindy: I've wanted to do a story on DJ's life for years, but I didn't know when or how to start. I mentioned it to Michael a few times, and finally he said, "Let's do it." So I started going over DJ's life in my head, and I was amazed by the journey we've been through together. Once I started to reflect, I had the opportunity to look back and think about all my trials, tribulations and accomplishments. When I first had DJ, I was just a regular mom raising my children with my husband. I thought I had it all figured out and was going to live my life the way I planned it.

Then all of a sudden, DJ was diagnosed with autism, and my life changed forever. I soon became a single mom raising a child with special needs. Raising DJ gave me the strength I didn't know I had or would ever need. Now I understand why my life needed a new direction. My old husband wasn't the man I was meant to marry forever. I'm glad I found out sooner rather than later. Once I remarried, I became a wife with five children, raising a child with special needs, in a loving family. So basically, this memoir helped me clear the air about a lot of things and gave me a new perspective on life. I get to be a proud autism mom. I just hope I'm a good influence on other moms and dads who are going through the same journey I've been through.

Michael: This was a great writing experience, and I finally had a chance to look in my rearview mirror and enjoy the ride. DJ has been a blessing to me. He has raised my awareness on autism and life in general. I felt pretty shallow and lost before I became a father and married a great woman like Cindy. Now, I'm definitely in a better place. Of course, I'm not perfect. Reading this book gave me the chance to see some areas where I could improve. I am allowing myself to be judged by my reading audience, but ultimately, only God can truly judge me. I realize that now more than ever.

2) What's the difference between a regular parent and an autism parent?

Cindy: Great question! Let me start by saying that all moms rock, and I applaud any mother who is raising her children. It's not easy at all, especially in this day and age. As an autism mom, I face challenges that regular moms don't necessarily have to deal with. For example, my child has limited capabilities, and I have to constantly focus on his progress to ensure he's on the right path. I've had to deal with being abandoned by my spouse and other so-called family members who refused to accept DJ's condition. Also, insensitive people have made fun of DJ. There is a laundry list of things associated with having a child with autism. On the bright side, I get to see my child in a whole new light that another parent may not understand. Everything—I mean everything—my child does is a blessing. DJ has so much to offer, and watching him grow is really like putting the pieces of a puzzle together. I also know that DJ is going to need me for the rest of my life, so I guess that's bitter and sweet. On one hand, I'll always have DJ around to smother me with unconditional love. However, I'll likely be leaving this earth before DJ. A regular mom can raise her children and eventually let them fend for themselves. I will never be able to let DJ fend for himself. And even after I die, I will still have to wonder if DJ's going to be OK.

Michael: The good thing about my situation is that I was an autism dad before I was a regular dad. DJ was my first parental experience, and it prepared me to deal with my biological kids. Actually, I take that back. DJ may have started out on the wild side, but he eventually calmed down and became the sweetest kid I ever met or heard of.

My two youngest brats, I mean sons, present way more challenges then I ever experienced with DJ.

Maybe I was able to understand DJ more because of his condition. I never underestimated DJ or gave him more slack then necessary; I just understood him more. And to be honest, I probably gave my own mother more hell than DJ ever gave me. So I guess the difference between being an autism dad and a regular dad is the level of understanding and patience that you have for your child.

3) Do you have any parental advice?

Cindy: Love your children unconditionally. I know that's easier said than done, especially when they grow up and get on your last nerve. (You'd have to be a long-term parent to understand.)

The best advice I can give any parent is to see the beauty in all their children. I don't care if you have one kid or one hundred kids. Always make each child feel like they have a part of you that only they own.

Michael: My best advice to any parent is to never give up. Don't even consider giving up as an option. I think some fathers feel that their role as a parent isn't as important as the mother's role. Nothing could be further from the truth. A father sets the tone for guidelines and structure in the home. Not to mention, it's the father's role to be the protector of the household so the mother can feel safe to nurture the kids properly.

4) Where do you see DJ in the future?

Cindy: To be honest, I don't really focus on DJ's future; I'm too busy living in the moment. It's hard to predict what DJ's future will be like because I don't know in which direction his autism spectrum will go. I'd like to say I'll see DJ with a nice paying job, a wife, kids, and a family of his own, but that doesn't seem realistic right now. For starters, DJ may be a bright boy and he's excellent with chores around the house, but I'm not sure if he'll ever have the mental capability to work for an employer or around other coworkers in a real workplace environment. DJ likes to do what DJ likes to do, and I don't want to have him being pressured to do work that he's not interested in or simply can't handle. As far as getting married and having kids, I can't imagine DJ in a serious intimate relationship. Michael actually brought this up a few months ago, and I was surprised I'd never thought about it before. But thinking out loud, I don't think I'll ever be comfortable with DJ being sexually active unless he demonstrates a higher level of comprehension and is able to express himself verbally. I hope I don't sound too overprotective, but that's just how I feel. I'm actually more worried about what will happen to DJ after I'm gone, but I try not to focus on that, either. Hopefully, DJ's future is a carefree existence that's filled with happy moments. That's the best I could wish for him at this point.

Michael: I was joking with Cindy about DJ having a girlfriend that looked like Beyoncé one day. When I noticed the look on Cindy's face, it dawned on me that this may be a very touchy subject for her. Right now, DJ's just an innocent twelve-year-old boy, and sexual relationships are out of the equation. However, DJ will become a man one day and still may never have the opportunity to have a real girlfriend, go out on dates, or have a wife and kids. I think it's most fathers' dream to see their sons chasing girls, having fun, and then settling down with the person they chose to marry. I know I look forward to my youngest son's escapades. This may sound like a double-standard, but I guess I have to look at DJ's situation differently. After all, I wouldn't want DJ in the hands of some random chick taking advantage of him. Time will tell if DJ's ever ready for that type of future. Meanwhile, I can picture DJ being a model for clothes, and even a poster boy for autism awareness. He definitely has the look.

5) Do you feel that enough is being done to promote medical research for autism and ASD awareness in general?

Michael: Maybe, I dunno. One out of sixty-eight children are being diagnosed with autism spectrum disorder; every year. But I don't know if doctors are diagnosing autism faster and more efficiently, or if more children are actually being born somewhere on the spectrum. In any case, I don't see a cure coming anytime soon. I think there are too many types of autism to pinpoint a particular cure. As far as awareness, I think more people have awareness these days. Now we need to embrace autism acceptance as well.

Cindy: I doubt it. I don't think there's a great demand for any serious autism cure. I get approached by a lot of witch doctors and so-called experts claiming they have a special formula or pill that cures autism. But if I allowed DJ to be diagnosed and treated by every Internet physician with a kooky medical hypothesis, I'd be putting DJ's health at risk. DJ's fine the way he is, and I don't feel he necessarily needs a cure. I will admit I would love to hear my son talk one day. I'm sure if he's meant to speak, it will happen naturally. I do feel that autism awareness is at an all-time high. It definitely has improved a lot in the last ten years or so.

6) What do you think about SB277 in California?

Cindy: I think it's a very insensitive bill. It's really a slap in the face to all the parents who have had their children die from vaccinations. And I'm not being biased because of DJ's situation. To be honest, I don't know for sure if vaccinations caused DJ's condition. I can only speculate. Still and all, I think allowing parents to exempt their child from certain vaccinations has been effective for years, and

I personally don't see why these shots should become mandatory now.

Michael: I pretty much agree with Cindy. However, I don't think the committee that came up with this bill intended to be insensitive or malicious. There are some concerned parents who urged this bill because they were afraid their children would catch a disease from an unvaccinated student. BUT, forcing every child to get vaccinated still doesn't guarantee that child a safe environment. Think about it: Even if you separate the vaccinated and unvaccinated at schools, these same kids will end up playing with one another in other public settings, so what are you gonna' do? Have separate societies for vaccinated and unvaccinated people? I think this bill has the potential to become dangerous, and I hope it doesn't reach other parts of the United States.

7) What do you hope to accomplish by writing this memoir?

Michael: I hope people will enjoy our story and use whatever insight they gained from reading it. I wanted us to write a book that was about our son's autism, but also our lives in general. I've read a few books on autism, and I noticed that some of them are too focused on all the negative aspects of ASD. I didn't want this book to be focused on a cure or have a depressing tone. Don't get me wrong—I understand that this can be a sensitive topic and some things about it are depressing. In the end, I wanted this book to be a celebration of our son and a tribute to all the kids and adults who have autism.

Cindy: Hopefully this book will be an inspiration to other parents who are raising a child with autism. I also hope this helps spread autism awareness as well as autism acceptance.

Will there be a "That's My DJ" part 2?

Michael: ...No

Cindy: LOL, Don't listen to Michael. There may be a part two. We haven't really looked that far ahead yet. Since DJ's turning thirteen, we might write another memoir after his 20th birthday. Then we can discuss DJ's teenage years in part 2. But as of now, we are just glad we were able to write this book.

Acknowledgments

———————

THANK YOU FOR READING OUR family journey. Writing "That's My DJ" has been one our best accomplishments!

Cindy- I would like to thank my wonderful son DJ for being an inspiration to write this book. I will be here for you until the end of time… You are the most special person on this earth as far as I'm concerned. I would also like to thank my children Imani, Nia, Malachi and Malik for making me feel like a super mom even when I was at my weakest point. I especially want to thank Imani for being my rock and one of my best friends. I love all my children with all my heart.

Thank you Tonya for being my little sister and my closest confidant, I really enjoyed your chapter in this book.

To my "futuristic candy bar" and love of my life Michael… From the moment we met it's been about the love we have for each other. Even when you were traveling the world I could feel you close to my heart.

I can't imagine trying to write this book alone... You are my hero and I want to spend the rest of my life in your arms....I hope your blushing... lol

And thank you Past Wiggins for marrying us. You were a good man and a very generous pastor, may you R.I.P

I would also like to thank my mother Noreen, my little brother Ryan, Aunt Margaret in Barbados, My Granny Ina for shaping my life and getting me in the right direction (you are so appreciated). Uncle First, Shemila Scantlebury- Johnson, Uncle Winston(R.I.P), Ave Belgrave, Aunty Janice, Simone Richards and her husband Ryan, Shelly, Creola and Ron Portious, Toya, Vonetta Calander, Denise Cater, Nicole Belgrave, Tammy Evelyn, Tonya Forde, Trevor Smith, DJ's Godmother Michelle Ball, Emily Riley from Special Olympics, Lauren Kidder(senior coordinator for Autism Speaks), Kelli Gold-Vendler, Vanetta Corbin (and her twins Jalisa and Jamelia), Jennifer Smith, Marjorie Mathieu, Victorine Topppin–Beckles, Joel Guerrier, Precious Brown, Nicki Jones, Donald Belgrave, Anya Loanis, Marva Smith, Harvey Smith, Joe Smith, Marva and Earl Lewis, Candice Can-Can Owens, Rashawn, Vince, Raoul Waithe, Amanda Shumski, Steven Jackson, Sophia Belgrave, Tamara Thomas, Shelia Riley, Taisha Mongomery, Robin Wiley, Ayonna, Ivy Turner, Charlotte Hinds (and her daughter Chyna), Ebony Hinds, Carlos Hinds, Castro, Donna Hinds, Mrs. Shelia, my girl Red, everyone at my job Olive Garden, Christine

Williams, Lena Isam, LaMonte Jenerette, Greg, Jennifer Burroff-Smith, Elliot, Jamie and Ashley Terry, Brooke, Bethany, Dustin, Courtney Kelly, Fera Toppins, Prisilla Gary, Cheyenne Atkins, Tyra Breaux, Princess Gary, Chauney Stephens, Jamal Snipes, Michael Roope, Wendy Pelmear, Daphne JeanBaptiste, Kristin Kramer, Brian Maystay, Antonio a.k.a Buck, Candace Blackstone, Angie Tarnick, Nicole Waterman, Maria Anthony, DJ's favorite teachers Mr. & Mrs. Lafave, Mr. Ryan (and most of the staff at Weddington Hills) Mrs. Tonja Okoye, Steven Cagle, Mrs. Carol, Latoya Dominique, Kathleen Anderson, DJ's doctor Dr. Morgan, DJ's Barber Chris at 5 Star Barbershop and thank you Toni Braxton for raising Diezel Ky Braxton-Lewis and being my inspiration as an Autism-mom (I may not know you in person but I relate to your journey)

To my online buddies that were kind enough to accept my friend request- Traci Forrest, Angela Suozzo-Shapiro, Marcia Hinds, Joy Brieske, Misty Garland Moler, Jennifer Joy-Ann, Heather Bowen-Walters, Stacy Marie, Yasmin Young and Vonyetta Lake with Power 98, No Limit Larry, J. Pragmatic, Najiyyah Mateen, Whitney Barnett, Robert Whithers, Jason Mac Nance, Lynn Holder, James Wynn, Tonisha Woodward, Charm Veney, Quina Robinson, April Barnett, Aida Donohue, June Cash, Khayree Pep C Fogle, Elise New Baucum, Daniel Svoboda, Angela Covington, Carol Adams, Kelly J. Bradshaw, Brianna Monroe, Michelle Leigh

Lashonda Clayton, Kazim Gomez, Trzecinski, Misley Ellis Mullen, Natalie Robison, Lisa Daley, Jes Sharky Filipski, Harmonie Lewis, Antoinette Faith Pope, Quamekia Shavers, Whitney Barnett, Melody Joy Rain, Whitney Hall, Ashlee Nolan, Allison Price Bard, Aiesha Baker, A'kasha Johnson, Daniel Svoboda, Cindy Sharp, Grace Mitchell, Harry Shaw Jr, Delisa Cooper, Angelique Emmanuel, Lynette Wadworth, Cassandra Johnson, Luckie Charm, Carol Adams, Barbarella Plaza Rogers, Katrina Cubean, Kelly Dodge ...and many, many more! R.I.P Dr. Bradstreet.

The autism groups: Autism Society of North Carolina, Autism Support Network, Autism Speaks, Asperger Syndrome Awareness, THE AUTISM FILE MAGAZINE, Autism: We are a Race not a Disease, Autism Black Fathers and Mothers United Connection- A.F.A.M.U.C., Autism rocks, Ladonna Jordan and the GFT group and many, many more... Thank you for letting me post.

I really just want to thank all the autism parents and people that support Autism Awareness.

Thank you D. Crowe for editing TMDJ

Michael- I'd like to thank God for giving me the courage to face another day. I often get in my moods and life gets hard but somehow I still manage to see the sun. I'm very thankful for my beautiful family and the love of my life Cindy. I can't even imagine what dark alley I would be laying in if you didn't save me. I may joke around about you chasing me but best believe I was never running. You are the only reason my life has balance. I want to acknowledge all my kids and pray for their safe journey in life. Imani, you have been one of my best friends and held me down on numerous occasions... I taught you how to drive a car and you taught me how to have drive in life... You are truly a blessing. To my little fly girl Nia... I have watched you grow from a spoiled princess to a beautiful Nubian queen and I keep wondering how one girl can have soo much talent. You are going to be a famous artist one day, I can feel it. To my first born Malachi, thank you for teaching me about dinosaurs and taking me to see Jurassic Park... I feel like you introduced me to a world that I never really understood. And my little spoiled brat Malik... Man, I should have never named you "King"... You have been trying to boss me around ever since. But I know you love your old man so I just roll with it. And DJ, my sonlight... I still can't believe God could make such a handsome, loving and sweet person. Because of you my life has purpose. When everybody else is off doing their own thing I can always count on you to hang with me. I may not hear you speak but because of you my heart grew a pair of ears.... And those dance moves you got make me want to show the world that you're my DJ!

Also, thank you Dad (O'Conney Mayhew) for teaching me how to be a father and always being there for me and congratulation to you and your beautiful wife Alfretta for 28 years of marriage. Now that's what I call an example of love everlasting. Feel better Grandma Daphne.

Thank you Yoomi and Yennoco for being the best sisters a brother could ever have, and their friends Naim, Raven and April. To my uncles and aunts thank you for your love and support, Aunt Pat, Uncle Chris, Aunt Rita, Uncle Lamont, Uncle Rex, Aunt Jackie, Aunt Jerry, Uncle Henry, Aunt Jane in Barbados, and rest in peace to my favorite Uncle Charlie... (we talk almost every day). And a special, special thanks to my beautiful Aunt Melissa for always believing in me and never letting me down. There's just way too much I can say... I'll have to write a book about you one day. Shout out to her husband Terrance as well. To all my big cousins and little cousins spread across the United States, I want to thank you for being there for me when I need you most, Shout out to cousin Tammy, Robby, Tawanna, Ninketa, Josel, Dennis, Donna, Fatiyah, Renee, Tammy, Angela, Ouincy, Sean, Danielle, Janae, Terrell, Jamal, Billy, Josh, Sonya, Nicole, Christina, Chucky, Emily, Portia, Yolanda (and her mother Aunt Edie), Felecia, Tamilia, Netta, Vanessa in Barbados, and others. R.I.P Bruce Washington.

And Jessica (my God sister), Tia, Erica, Sarah, Sam Linda, Fran, R.I.P Glady's, Jimmy and Ruby.

I'd like to show my appreciation to all my Merchant Marine buddies (keep cruising that salt water...the world is yours). I see you Kedra Turner! To my personal childhood friends, Mulley Mac, Nijer, Yasha, Tracey, Lamar Morton, Goff J-crush Phillips, Nikia Haskell, Larry a.k.a Face, Lutha, Sko, Shanta, Lorraine Berry, Mike Berry, Aiesha Hammond, Lefty, Taneika, Lasandra, Camille, Daryl, Doughboy, Chad, all of N. Munn Avenue. And my co-workers at G4S, Virona Vee Johnson (thanks a million beautiful), Ed Hendrickson, Mr. Gregory, Steve Dorn a.k.a (Mr. Long Island!), Bobby Fee, Tony, Shemelle, Sasha, Jamal, Freweini, Brandi, Greg, Yvonne, Tre (my right hand man), Denise, Jeff, Jason, Dorethea, Enoch, Randolpho, Juan, Christy, Dee, Jamal, Raheim, Neff, Solomon, Lorenzo, Maya, Shamain, Nessa, Rahj, Marlon, Jarret, Charlie, Saane, Melinda, Blair, Jennifer, Artist, Emily Leigh, Serge and his wife Lorraine

David, Prince, Crazy Eddie, Ben (my prayer buddy), The Metlife Woodward and Gragg Building staff, and whoever I forgot from the bottom of my heart thank you..

I want to also thank my O.D.A.T boys for having my back! ShockDoc, SkullyBoy, Bird, Philly, SP, Reek Exquisite Red, My Big Homie Ray-Dog and the rest of the team… (way too many to name)

Everyone at 5 Star Barbershop, Chris, Jacques, K from Brooklyn, Pete, James, Curtis Ronnie, Jamarquis

Thank you to all the social media sites and Facebook friends that took the time to read "That's My DJ" when it was just a manuscript… Especially June Cash, Ebony Hinds, Cassandra Henderson. Jason Kerr, Tre Green, Yvonne Williams

Your feedback was very helpful

And last but not least, my beautiful mother Pamela J. Mayhew. I don't think I can type too much without crying so I'll just say thank you for all your love and I pray you get better… I'll be at the rehabilitation center to read you your copy of "That's My DJ"… I know this book's going to make you smile

THANK YOU FOR GETTING
MY BOOK. I WOULD LOVE TO
SIGN YOUR COPY. PLEASE BE
PATIENT WITH ME AND I WILL
SPELL MY NICK NAME 4 U.

HAVE A GREAT DAY!!!

Yours Truly,
Desmond "DJ" Joseph

X _____

Contact:

PIIAB PUBLISHING

1-704-701-3649
1-980-253-7772
MMAYHEW0@EMAIL.CPCC.EDU

Made in the USA
Charleston, SC
21 October 2015